Read
Trace
Write

a
એક

I
હું

am
છું

an
એક

as
જેમ કે

at
પર

AF442137

Read and write the sentence!

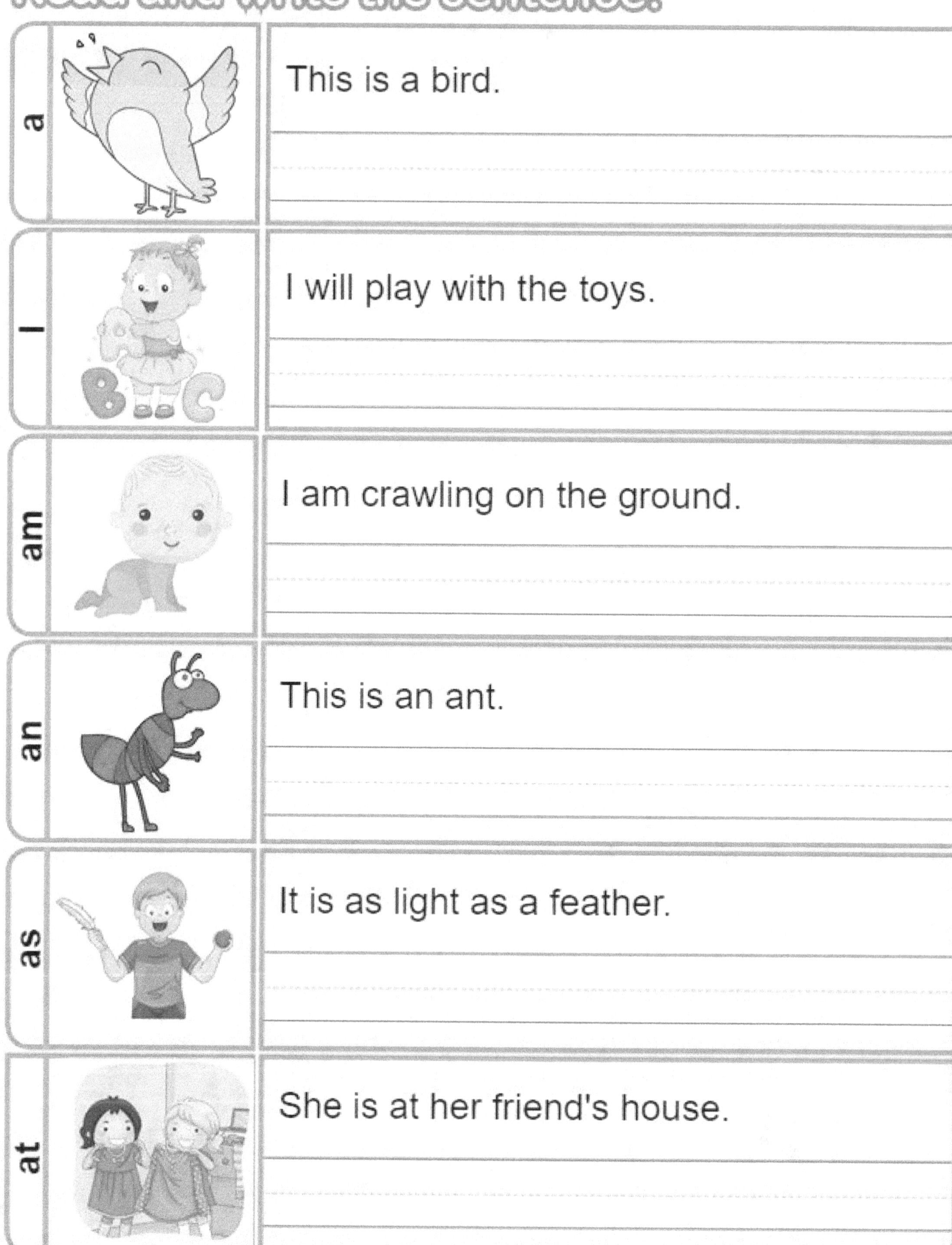

a		This is a bird.
I		I will play with the toys.
am		I am crawling on the ground.
an		This is an ant.
as		It is as light as a feather.
at		She is at her friend's house.

Read   Trace   Write

Read	Trace	Write
be હોઇ		
by દ્વારા		
do કરવું		
go જાઓ		
he તેમને		
if જો		

Read and write the sentence!

be	We will be friends.
by	This story is by me.
do	She will do the cleaning.
go	He will go somewhere.
he	He is bored.
if	If I put my clothes here, it will get washed.

Read
Trace
Write
in
માં
is
છે
it
તે
me
મને
my
મારા
no
ના

Read and write the sentence!

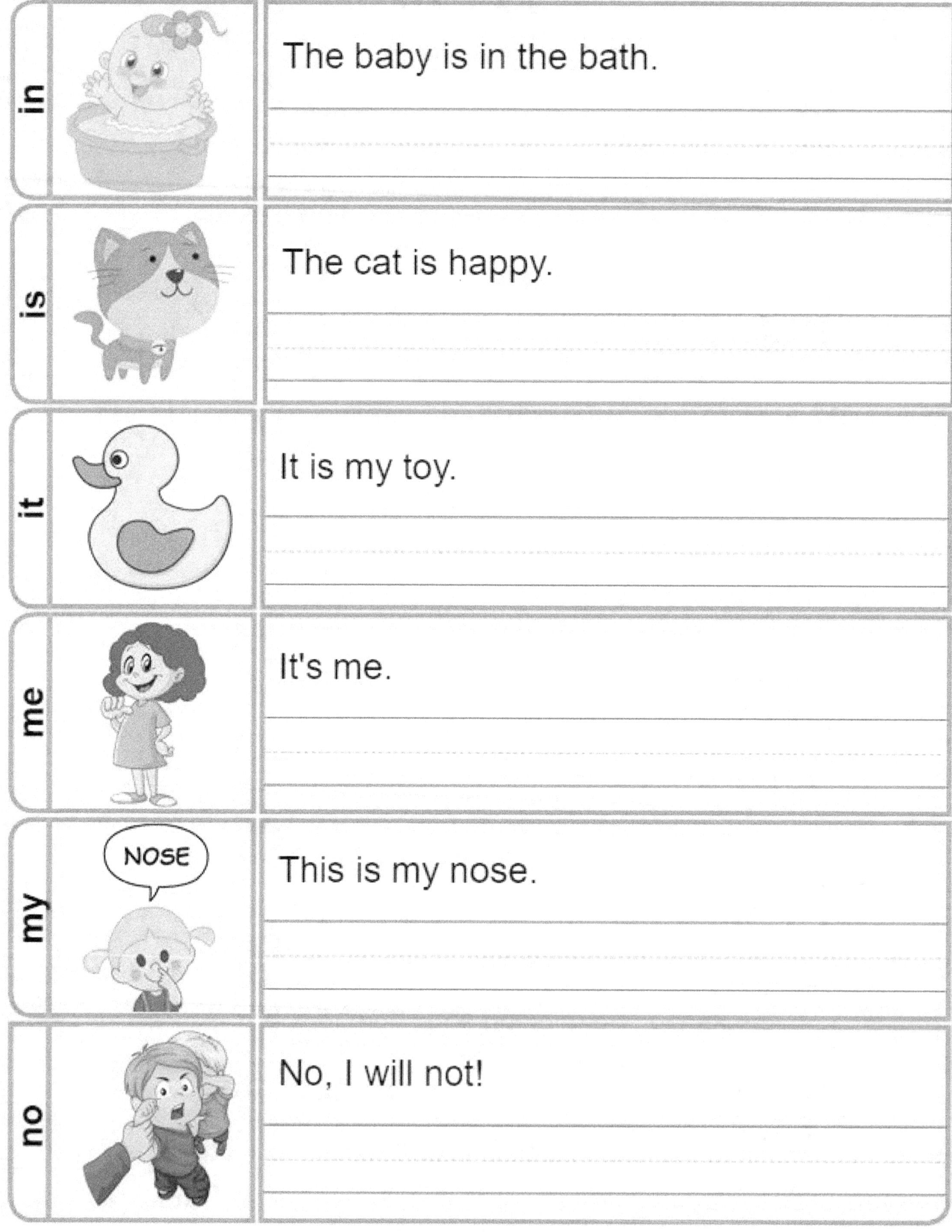

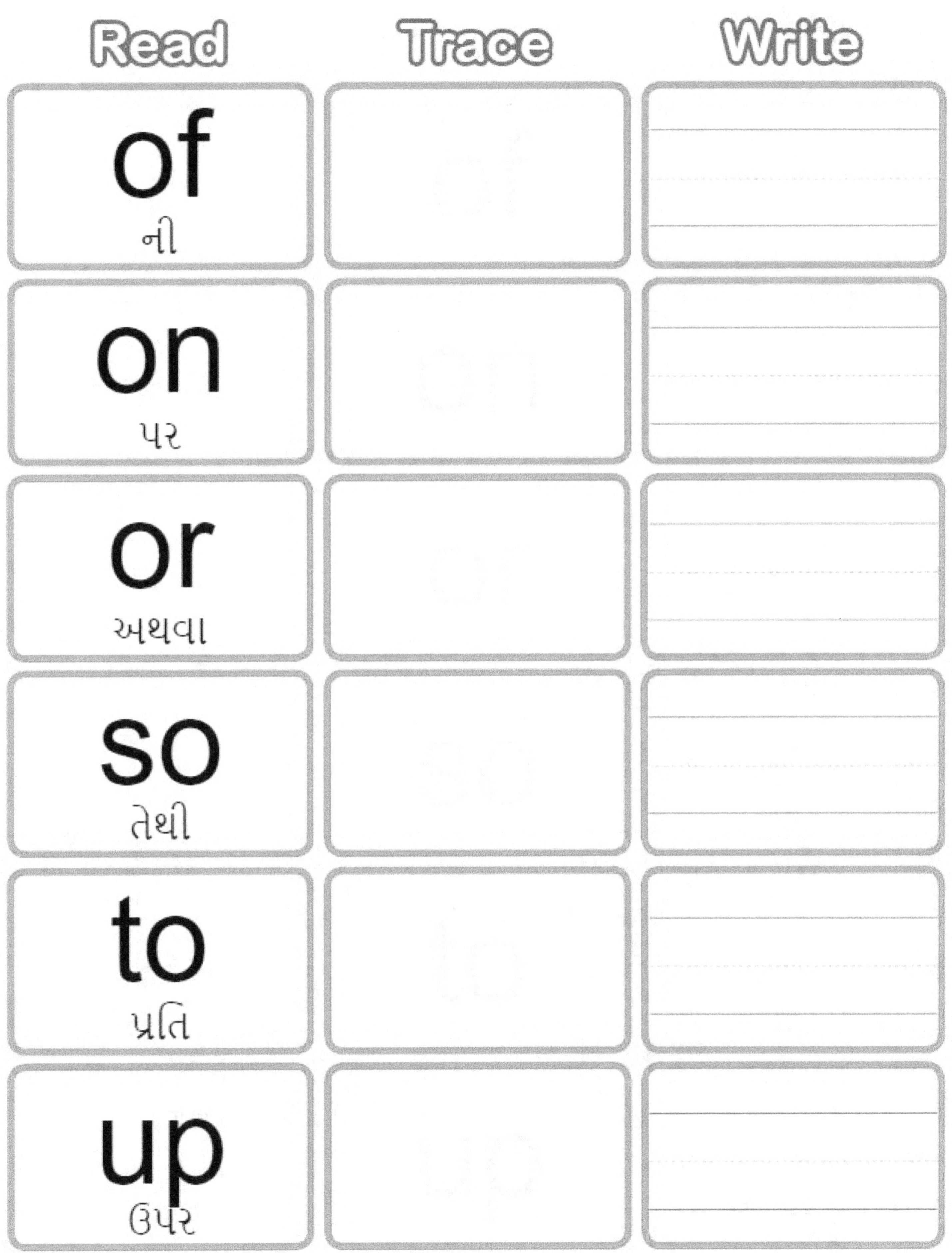

Read
Trace
Write
of
ની
on
પર
or
અથવા
so
તેથી
to
પ્રતિ
up
ઉપર

Read and write the sentence!

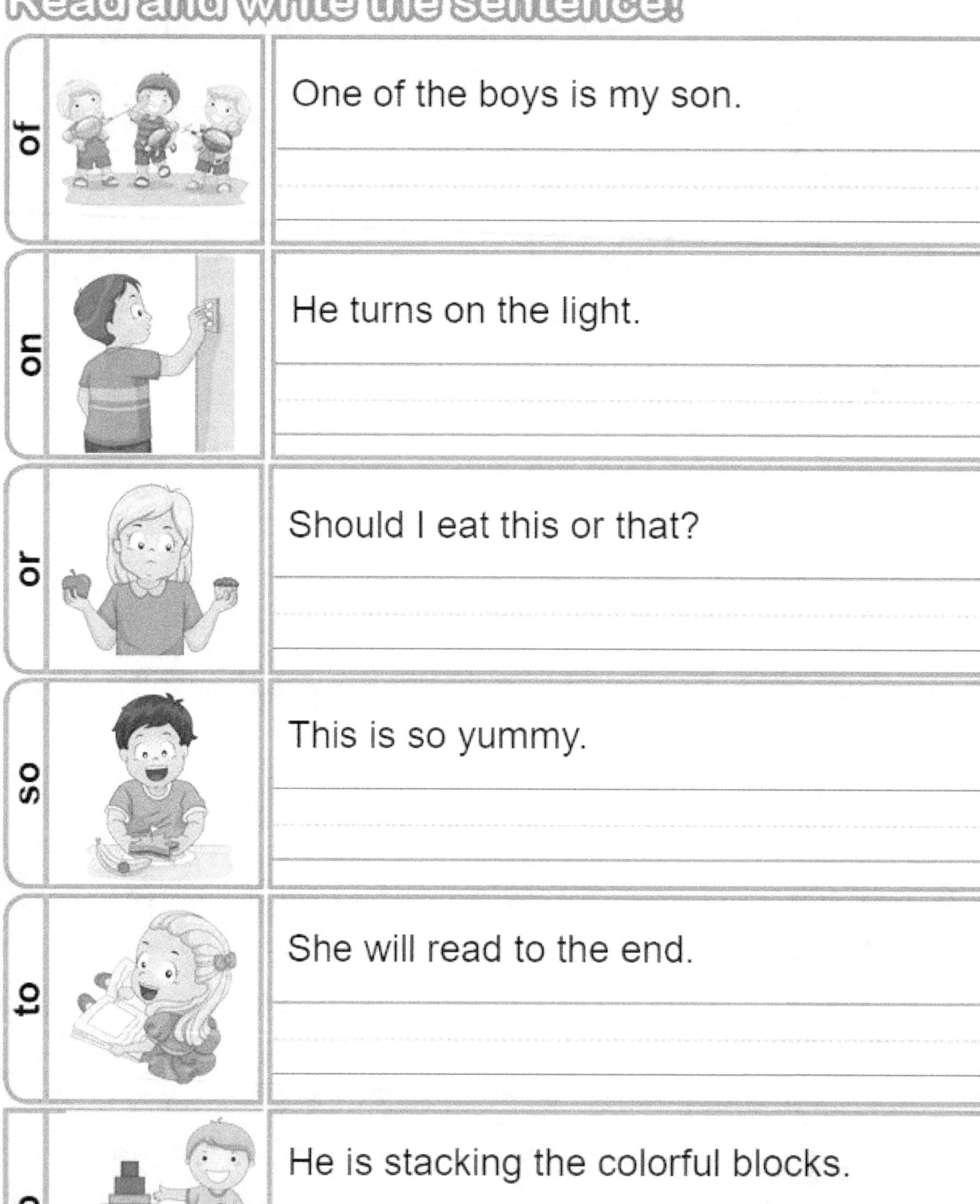

Read
Trace
Write
us
અમને
we
અમે
all
બધા
and
અને
any
કોઈપણ
are
છે

Read and write the sentence!

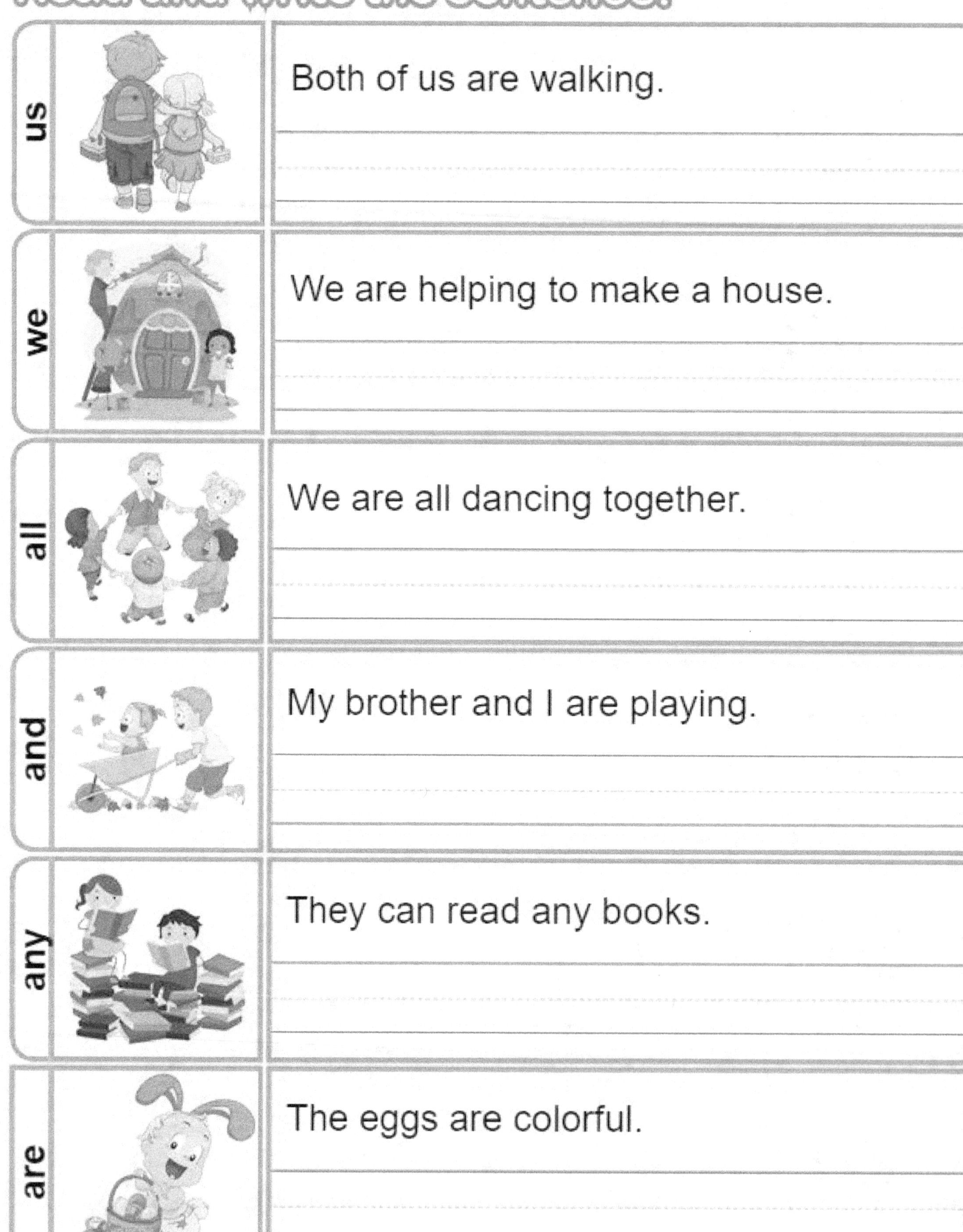

us	Both of us are walking.
we	We are helping to make a house.
all	We are all dancing together.
and	My brother and I are playing.
any	They can read any books.
are	The eggs are colorful.

Read   Trace   Write

Read and write the sentence!

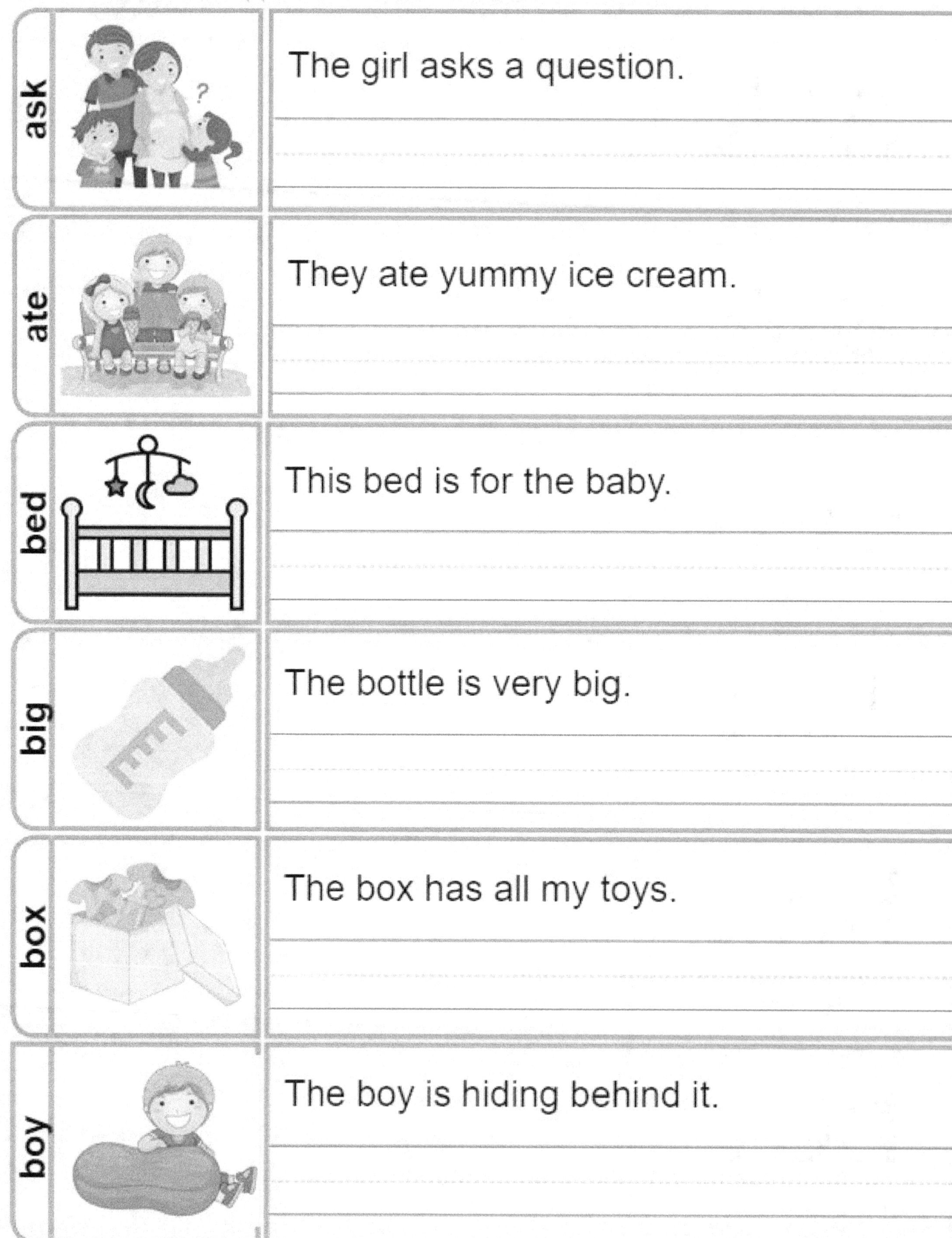

ask		The girl asks a question.
ate		They ate yummy ice cream.
bed		This bed is for the baby.
big		The bottle is very big.
box		The box has all my toys.
boy		The boy is hiding behind it.

Read
Trace
Write
but
પરંતુ
buy
ખરીદી
can
કરી શકો છો
car
કાર
cat
બિલાડી
cow
ગાય

Read and write the sentence!

but	I want to go, but my son doesn't.
buy	He buys lots of stuff.
can	The baby will drink milk from the can.
car	The car is red.
cat	The cat is sad.
cow	The cow is funny.

Read
Trace
Write

cut
કાપવું

day
દિવસ

did
કર્યું

dog
કૂતરો

eat
ખાવું

egg
ઇંડા

Read and write the sentence!

Read	Trace	Write
eye આંખ		
far દૂર		
fly ઉડાન		
for માટે		
get મેળવો		
got મળી		

Read and write the sentence!

Read
Trace
Write
had
હતી
has
છે
her
તેણીના
him
તેને
his
તેના
hot
ગરમ

Read and write the sentence!

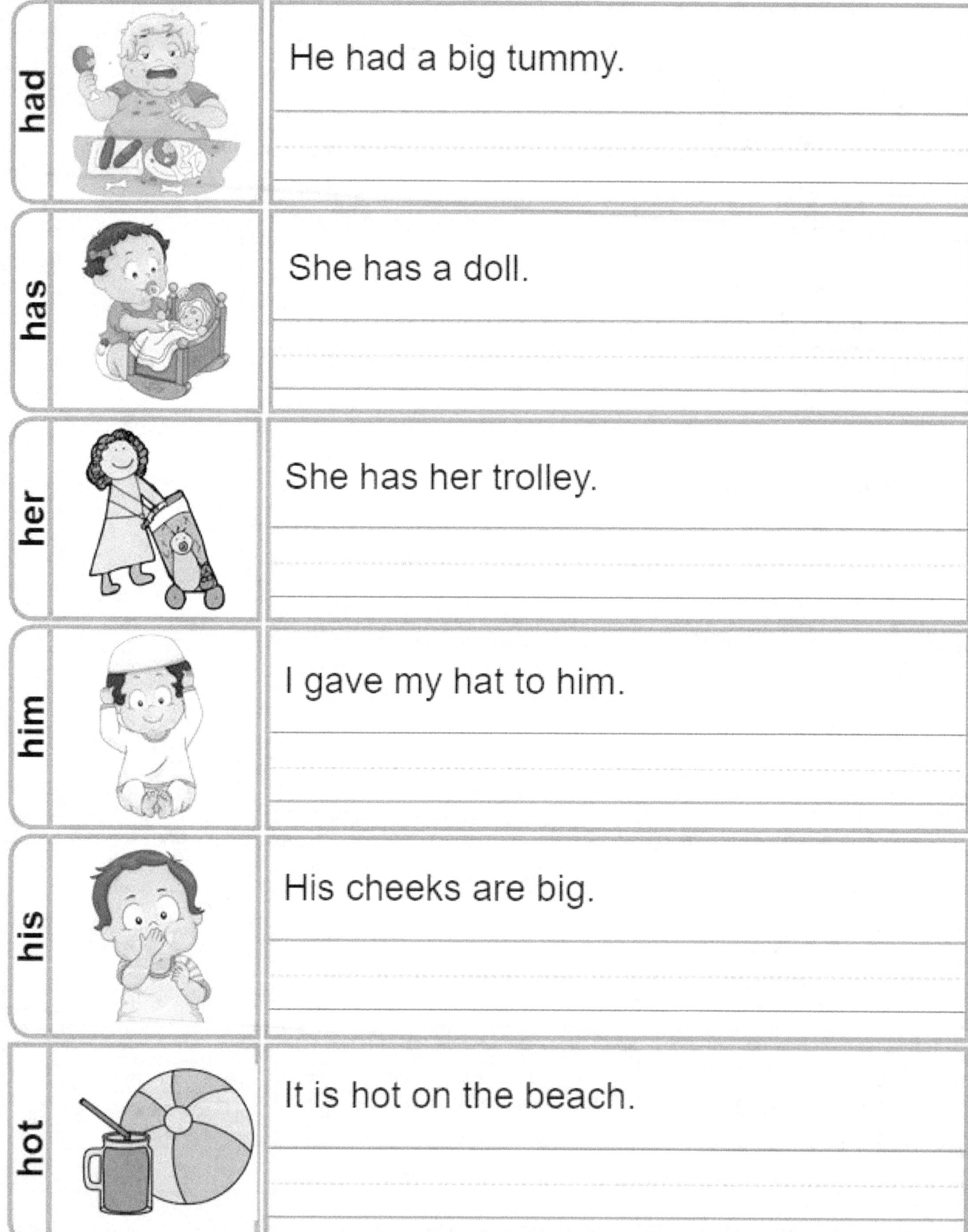

Read
Trace
Write
how
કેવી રીતે
its
તેના
leg
પગ
let
દો
man
માણસ
may
મે

Read and write the sentence!

how	How many blocks are there?
its	Its legs are short.
leg	His legs are short.
let	Let me come in!
man	The man is a vet.
may	May I have more?

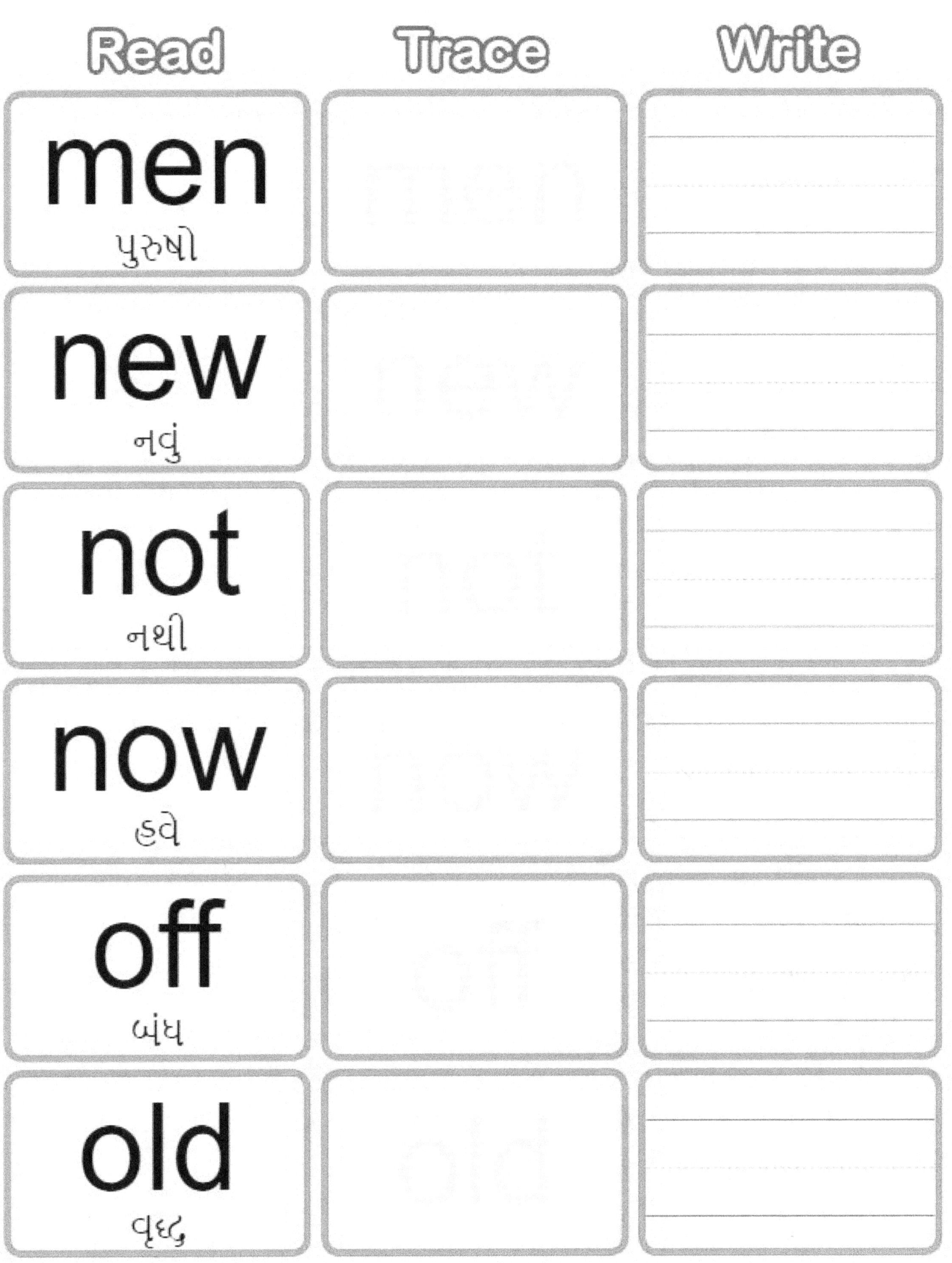

Read
Trace
Write
men
પુરુષો
new
નવું
not
નથી
now
હવે
off
બંધ
old
વૃદ્ધ

Read and write the sentence!

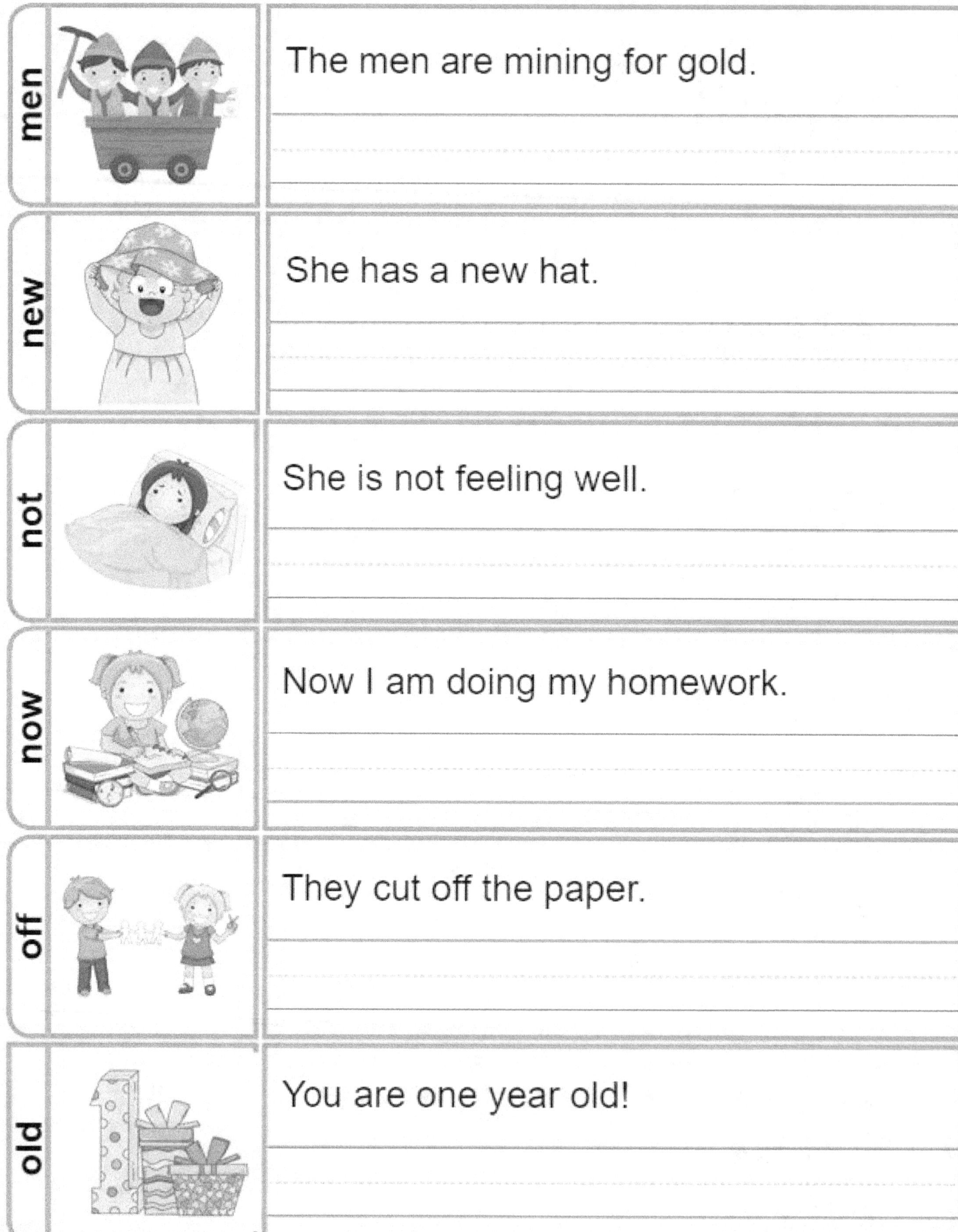

Read
Trace
Write
one
એક
our
અમારા
out
બહાર
own
પોતાના
pig
ડુક્કર
put
મૂકો

Read and write the sentence!

one		The panda says one.
our		This is our room.
out		He will go out.
own		The man owns a computer.
pig		She is sleeping on her pig.
put		She is putting an arm around her daughter.

Read
Trace
Write
ran
ચલાવો
red
લાલ
run
ચલાવો
saw
જુઓ
say
કહો
see
જુઓ

Read and write the sentence!

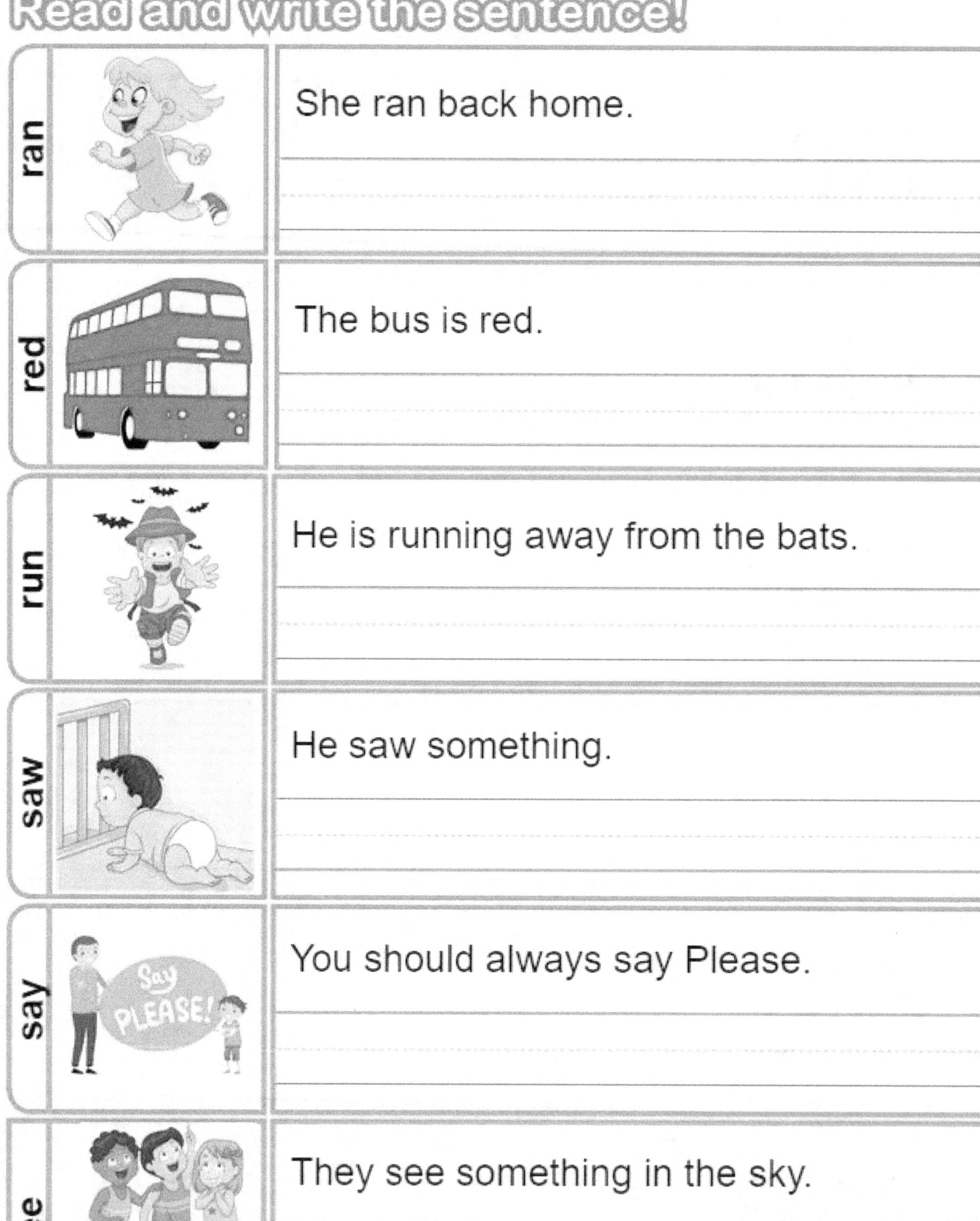

Read
Trace
Write
she
તે
sit
બેસવું
six
છ
sun
સૂર્ય
ten
દસ
the
એક

Read and write the sentence!

Read
Trace
Write
too
પણ
top
ટોચ
toy
રમકડું
try
પ્રયાસ કરો
two
બે
use
વાપરવુ

Read and write the sentence!

too
The bear is too cute.

top
The pot is on the top.

toy
The baby has lots of toys.

try
We try to be kind to him.

two
Today you have turned two.

use
I use my toothpaste and toothbrush.

Read
Trace
Write
was
હતી
way
માર્ગ
who
શું
why
શા માટે
yes
હા
you
તમે

Read and write the sentence!

was	He was reading a book.
way	Let's go this way
who	Who wants to dance?
why	Why is the machine not working?
yes	Yes, I am so happy!
you	I love you!

Read
Trace
Write

away
દૂર

baby
બાળક

back
પાછા

ball
દડો

bear
રીંછ

been
હતી

Read and write the sentence!

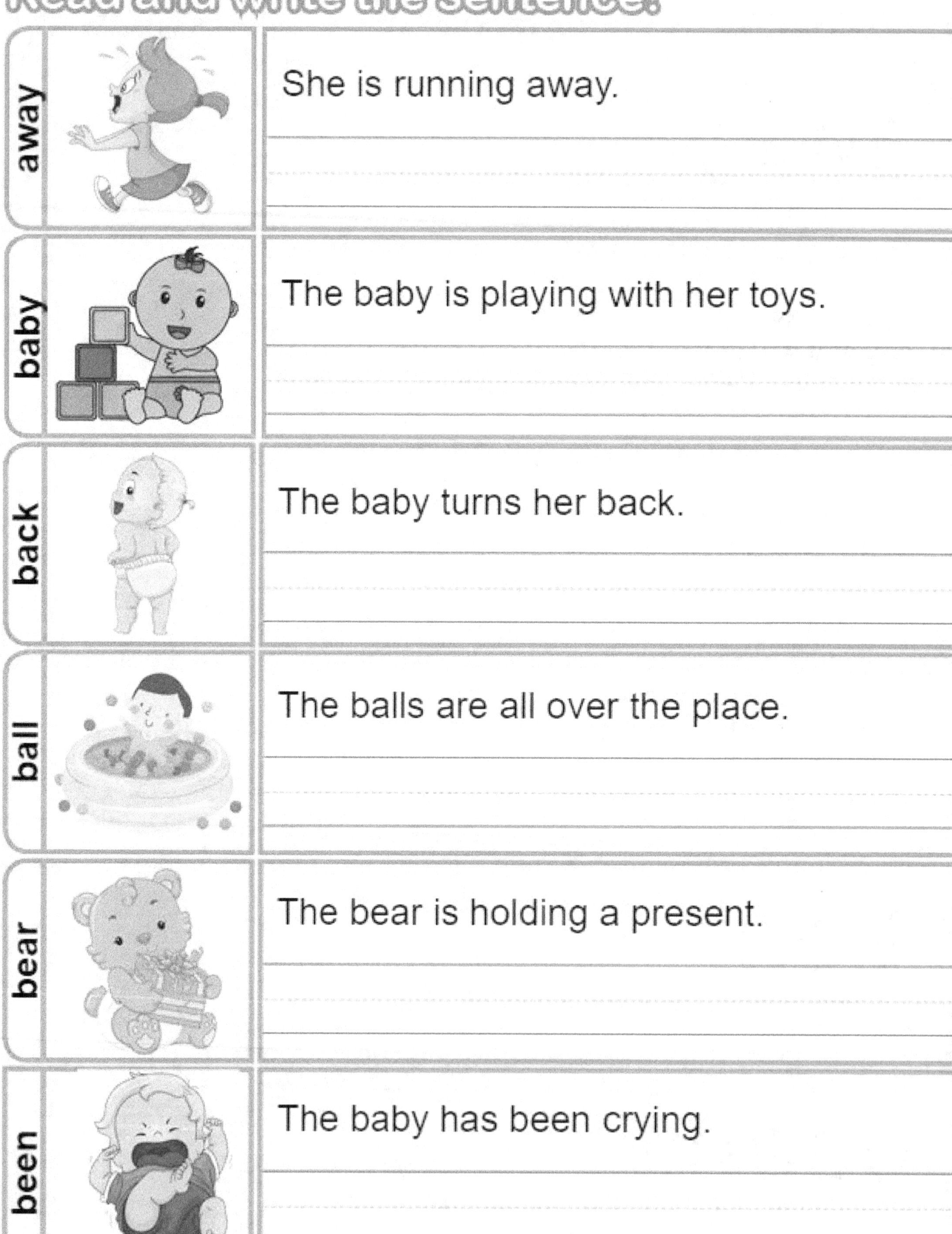

Read
Trace
Write

bell
ઘંટડી

best
શ્રેષ્ઠ

bird
પક્ષી

blue
વાદળી

boat
બોટ

both
બંને

Read and write the sentence!

bell	The bells are ringing.
best	This is the best food for babies.
bird	The bird is flying.
blue	The boy dressed up in blue.
boat	The boat will go into the ocean.
both	Both of you look so much alike.

Read
Trace
Write
cake
કેક
call
ક callલ કરો
came
આવ્યા
coat
કોટ
cold
ઠંડા
come
આવો

Read and write the sentence!

cake	The cake is for your birthday.
call	She is calling for somebody.
came	She came with her bag.
coat	The girl is wearing her coat.
cold	The baby feels cold.
come	Come here to the slide!

Read
Trace
Write
corn
મકાઈ
does
કરે છે
doll
doઈગલી
done
થઈ ગયું
door
દરવાજો
down
નીચે

Read and write the sentence!

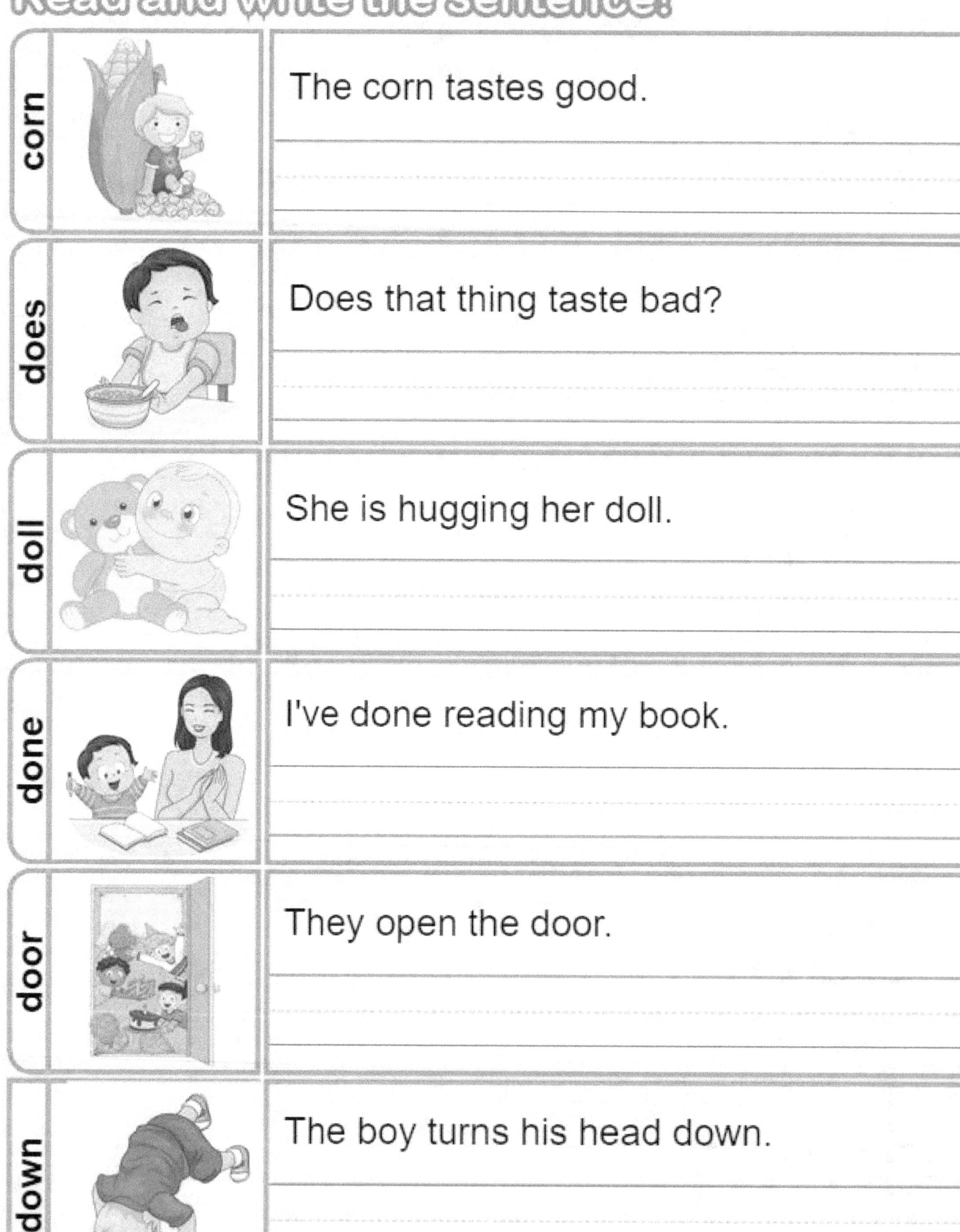

corn	The corn tastes good.
does	Does that thing taste bad?
doll	She is hugging her doll.
done	I've done reading my book.
door	They open the door.
down	The boy turns his head down.

Read	Trace	Write
draw દોરો		
duck બતક		
fall પતન		
farm ફાર્મ		
fast ઝડપી		
feet પગ		

Read and write the sentence!

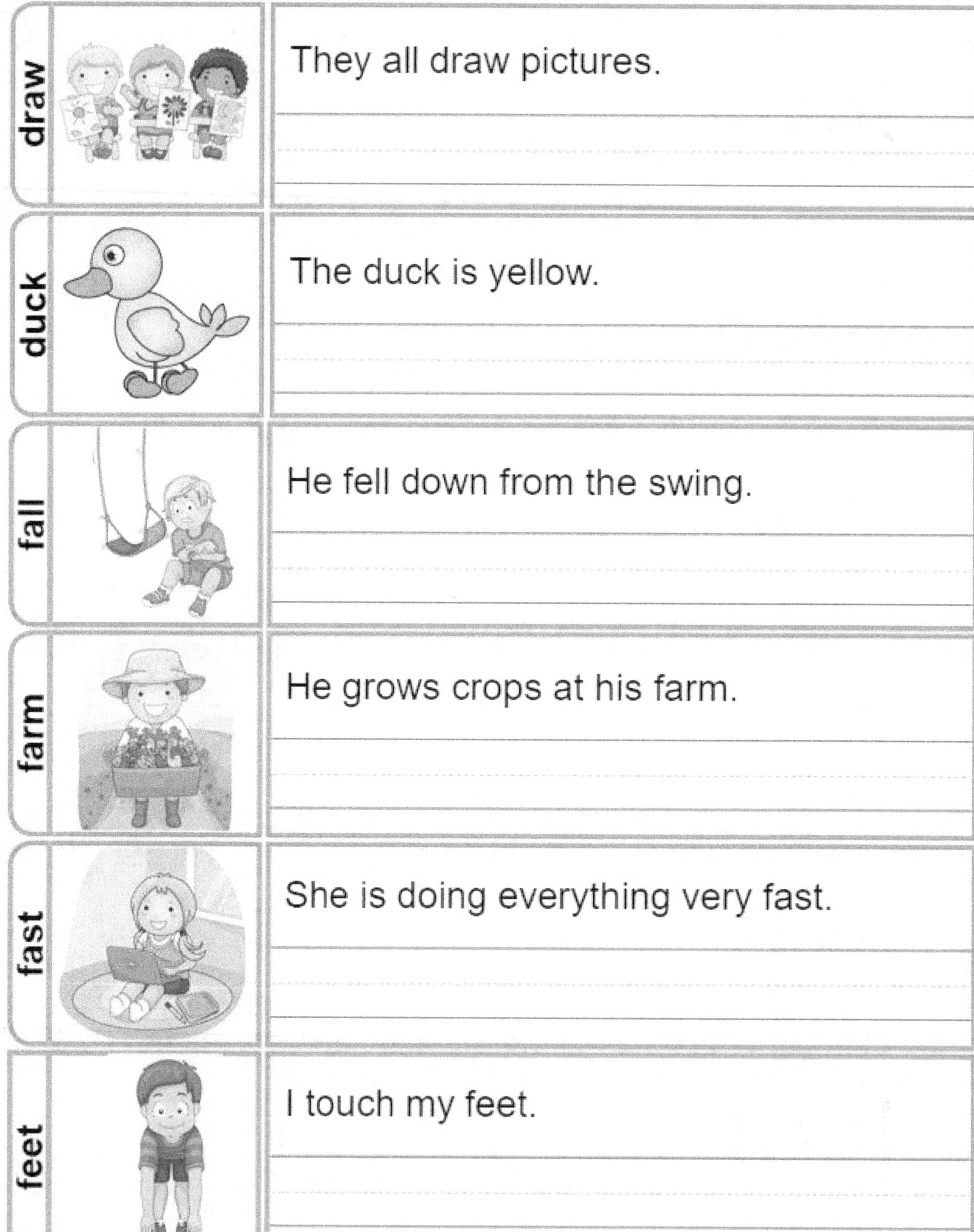

draw	They all draw pictures.
duck	The duck is yellow.
fall	He fell down from the swing.
farm	He grows crops at his farm.
fast	She is doing everything very fast.
feet	I touch my feet.

Read
Trace
Write
find
શોધો
fire
આગ
fish
માછલી
five
પાંચ
four
ચાર
from
માંથી

Read and write the sentence!

They are finding something.

The fire is blazing and dangerous.

The fish are swimming in the ocean.

You get birthday gifts for turning five.

The lion is turning four today.

She will draw a picture of her flower.

Read
Trace
Write
full
ભરેલું
game
રમત
gave
આપ્યો
girl
છોકરી
give
આપો
goes
જાય છે

Read and write the sentence!

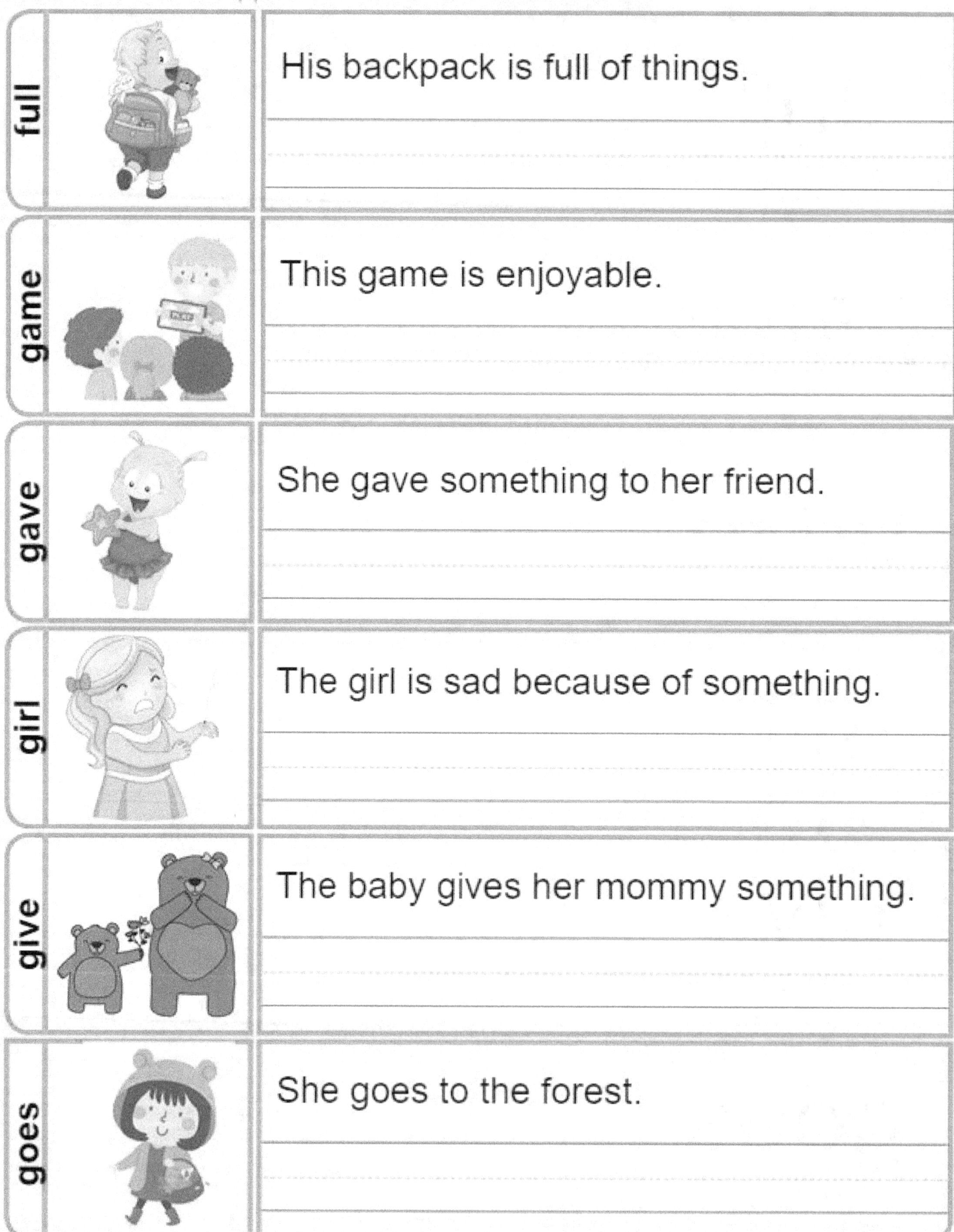

	Sentence
full	His backpack is full of things.
game	This game is enjoyable.
gave	She gave something to her friend.
girl	The girl is sad because of something.
give	The baby gives her mommy something.
goes	She goes to the forest.

Read	Trace	Write

good	The baby is acting very well today.
grow	My plant will grow!
hand	My hand is touching the wall.
have	She will have lots of friends.
head	My head is round.
help	They help each other wash the clothes.

Read	Trace	Write
here અહીં		
hill ટેકરી		
hold પકડી રાખવું		
home ઘર		
hurt નુકસાન		
into માં		

here		America is over here.
hill		The hill has some trees and a house.
hold		He is holding his daughter.
home		He drew a picture of his home.
hurt		The boy is hurt.
into		He will jump into the pool.

Read
Trace
Write
jump
કૂદી
just
માત્ર
keep
રાખવું
kind
દયાળુ
know
જાણો
like
ગમે છે

Read and write the sentence!

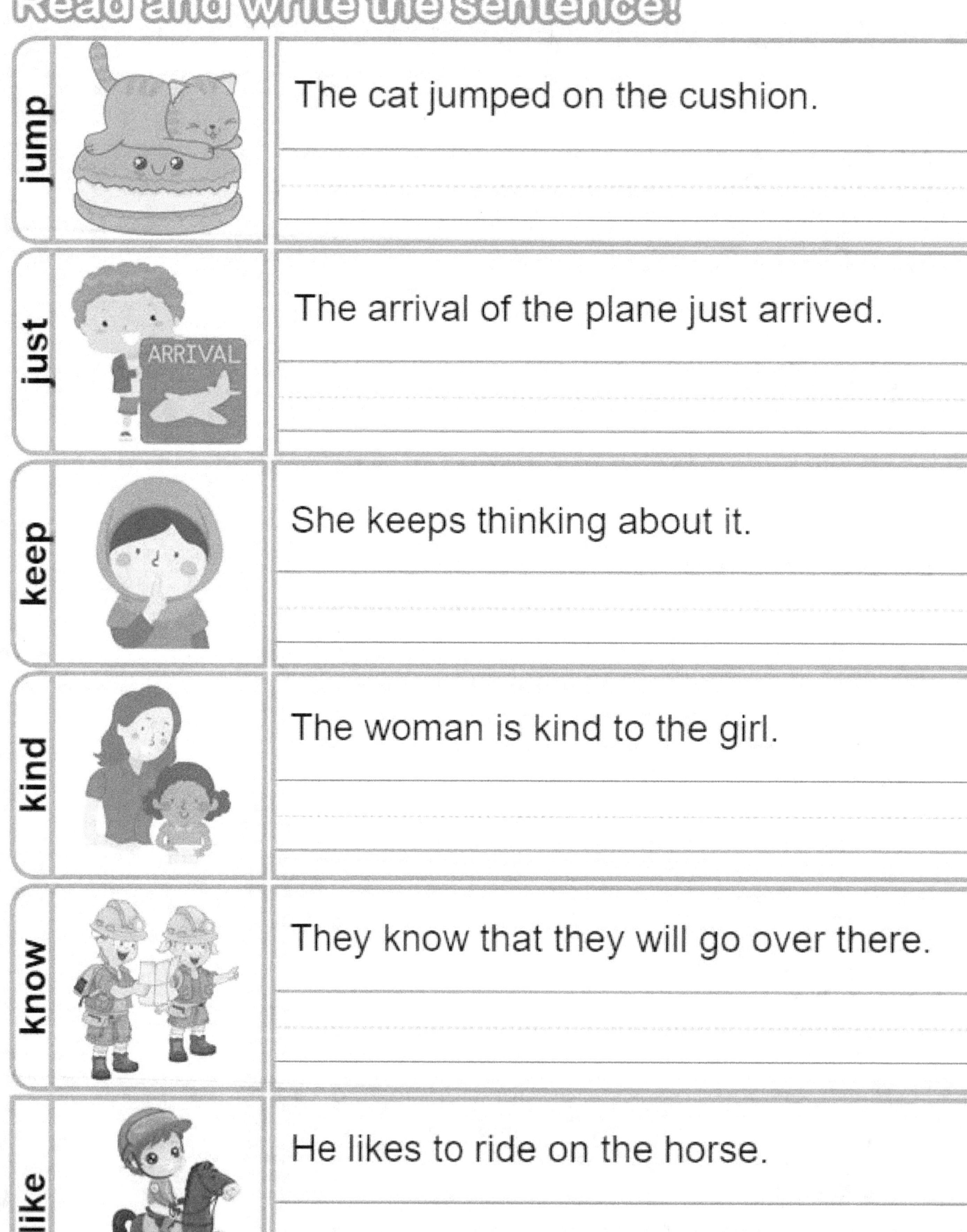

jump	The cat jumped on the cushion.
just	The arrival of the plane just arrived.
keep	She keeps thinking about it.
kind	The woman is kind to the girl.
know	They know that they will go over there.
like	He likes to ride on the horse.

Read
Trace
Write
live
જીવંત
long
લાંબી
look
જુઓ
made
બનાવેલું
make
બનાવેલું
many
ઘણા

Read and write the sentence!

live		They all live together.
long		The pencil is very long.
look		They are looking at something.
made		They made a promise.
make		They are going to make something.
many		He has many shirts.

Read
Trace
Write

milk
દૂધ

much
ઘણું

must
જ જોઇએ

name
નામ

nest
માળો

once
એકવાર

Read and write the sentence!

Read
Trace
Write
only
માત્ર
open
ખુલ્લા
over
ઉપર
pick
ચૂંટો
play
રમ
pull
ખેંચો

Read and write the sentence!

	Sentence
only	There is only one student.
open	He wants to open the door.
over	The class is over.
pick	She picked up something.
play	They like to play together.
pull	She is pulling on her friend's hair.

Read	Trace	Write
rain વરસાદ		
read વાંચવું		
ride રાઇડ		
ring રિંગ		
said કહ્યું		
seed બીજ		

Read and write the sentence!

rain	The rain is not going to hit us.
read	She likes to read books.
ride	The baby is riding on a toy horse.
ring	The bird is holding a ring in its beak.
said	She said hello to her neighbor.
seed	The seeds are going to plant.

Read
Trace
Write
shoe
જૂતા
show
બતાવો
sing
ગાઓ
snow
બરફ
some
કેટલાક
song
ગીત

Read and write the sentence!

shoe	Her shoes are cute and purple.
show	This map shows the location.
sing	The baby can sing along.
snow	I like to play snow.
some	These are some of my toys.
song	I will sing a song in the talent show.

Read
Trace
Write
soon
જલ્દી
stop
બંધ
take
લો
tell
કહો
that
કે
them
તેમને

Read and write the sentence!

soon		The eggs will hatch soon.
stop		The teacher says to stop.
take		They take some flowers.
tell		She is telling a story.
that		That bird dressed up as Santa.
them		He likes to eat them.

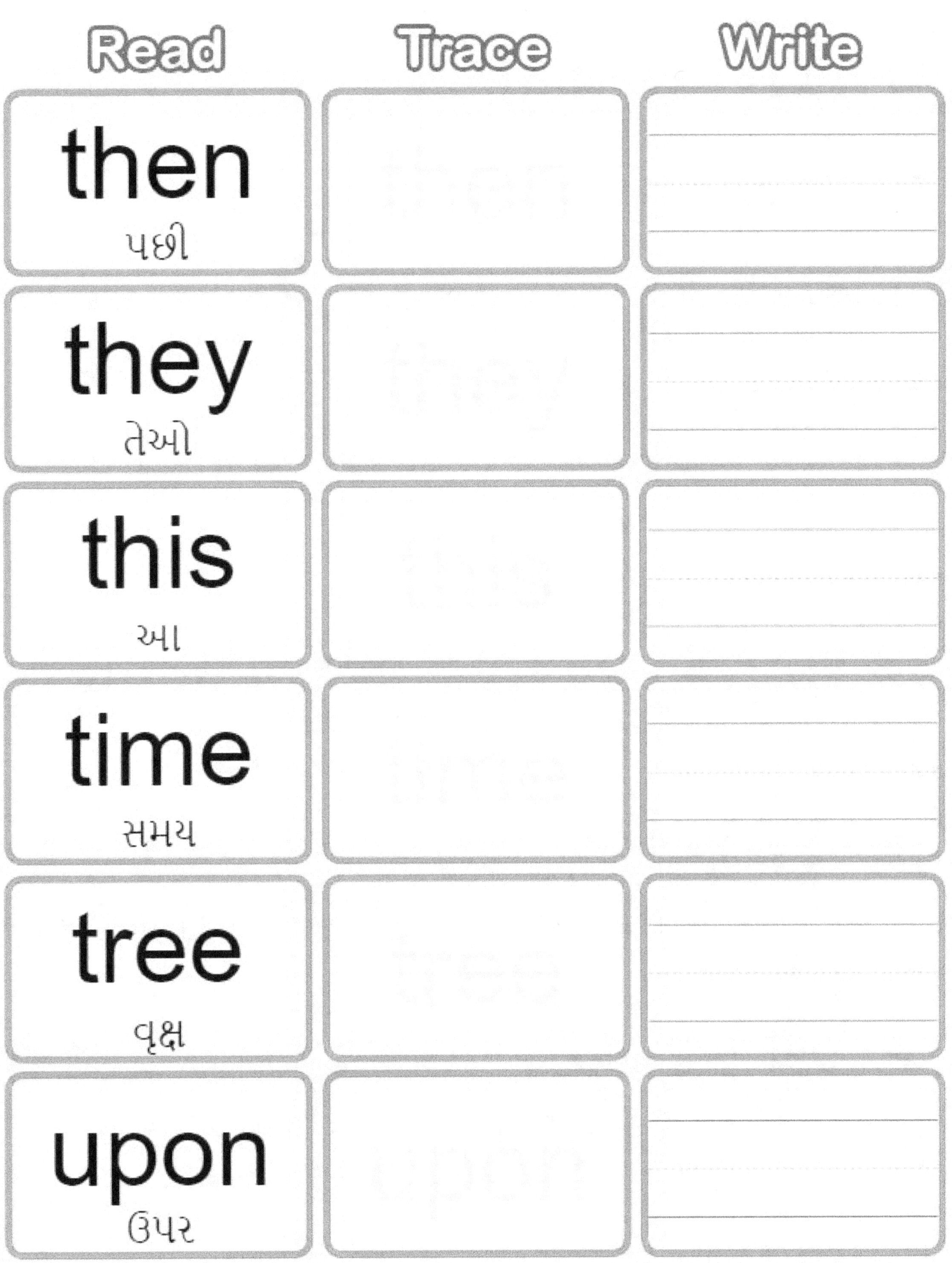

Read
Trace
Write
then
પછી
they
તેઓ
this
આ
time
સમય
tree
વૃક્ષ
upon
ઉપર

Read and write the sentence!

then	Then, I will go to bed.
they	They are running to school.
this	This is my duck.
time	The time always moves on.
tree	There are lots of green trees in the park.
upon	Once upon a time, there was a princess.

<table>
<tr><th>Read</th><th>Trace</th><th>Write</th></tr>
<tr><td>very
ખૂબ</td><td></td><td></td></tr>
<tr><td>walk
ચાલવા</td><td></td><td></td></tr>
<tr><td>want
જોઇએ છે</td><td></td><td></td></tr>
<tr><td>warm
ગરમ</td><td></td><td></td></tr>
<tr><td>wash
ધોવું</td><td></td><td></td></tr>
<tr><td>well
સારું</td><td></td><td></td></tr>
</table>

Read and write the sentence!

very	The baby is lovely.
walk	They are walking on the sidewalk.
want	The baby wants more milk.
warm	The bath is warm.
wash	She is going to wash the dishes.
well	He can save money well.

Read
Trace
Write
went
ગયા
were
છે
what
શું
when
ક્યારે
will
કરશે
wind
પવન

Read and write the sentence!

went	The crocodile went to the pond.
were	There were lots of toys.
what	What is the lion doing?
when	When are you going to wake up?
will	Will I get it in?
wind	The wind is blowing fiercely.

Read	Trace	Write
wish ઇચ્છા		
with સાથે		
wood લાકડું		
work કામ		
your તમારા		
about વિશે		

Read and write the sentence!

wish	I wish you a happy Christmas!
with	He is with his sister.
wood	He is stacking up wooden blocks.
work	He is going to work in his tractor.
your	Your baby is wearing a yellow suit.
about	It's about to be 12:30.

Read
Trace
Write
after
પછી
again
ફરી
apple
સફરજન
black
કાળો
bread
બ્રેડ
bring
લાવો

Read and write the sentence!

after		The teacher calmed them after they fought.
again		He did it again!
apple		The apple is red and juicy.
black		The crow is black.
bread		My breakfast is bread and jam.
bring		He is bringing his project.

Read
Trace
Write
brown
ભુરો
carry
વહન
chair
ખુરશી
clean
ચોખ્ખો
could
શકવું
don't
નહીં

brown — Her stuffed animal is a brown bear.

carry — He is carrying a big crayon.

chair — He is sitting on his chair.

clean — He needs to clean up.

could — The baby could do push-ups.

don't — Don't do that!

Read
Trace
Write
drink
પીવું
eight
આઠ
every
દરેક
first
પ્રથમ
floor
ફ્લોર
found
મળી

Read and write the sentence!

drink		The baby likes to drink water.
eight		You get eight gifts for turning eight!
every		Every book is colorful.
first		We won first place.
floor		She is sitting on the floor.
found		It found a hat in the streets.

Read
Trace
Write
funny
રમુજી
going
જાઓ
grass
ઘાસ
green
લીલા
horse
ઘોડો
house
ઘર

Read and write the sentence!

funny	The rabbit thinks the joke is funny.
going	The bear is going to eat all the honey.
grass	The goat eats grass on the hill.
green	The turtle that is walking is green.
horse	The horse is magical.
house	They lived in that house.

Read	Trace	Write
kitty બિલાડી		
laugh હસવું		
light પ્રકાશ		
money પૈસા		
never ક્યારેય		
night રાત્રે		

Read and write the sentence!

kitty	The kitties are charming.
laugh	They are laughing while playing.
light	The boy will turn on the lights.
money	I have earned a lot of money.
never	The bear never ate ice cream before.
night	I will sleep on my blanket at night.

Read
Trace
Write
paper
કાગળ
party
પાર્ટી
right
સાચું
round
ગોળ
seven
સાત
shall
કરશે

Read and write the sentence!

Read
Trace
Write
sheep
ઘેટાં
sleep
ઊંઘ
small
નાના
start
શરૂઆત
stick
લાકડીઓ
table
ટેબલ

Read and write the sentence!

Word		Sentence
sheep		The sheep have a bell around its neck.
sleep		I will go to sleep in my comfortable bed.
small		The small baby will crawl to its crib.
start		She will start sleeping soon.
stick		He has some sticks to play.
table		The table has a toy on it.

Read
Trace
Write
thank
આભાર
their
તેમના
there
ત્યાં
these
આ
thing
વસ્તુ
think
વિચારો

thank	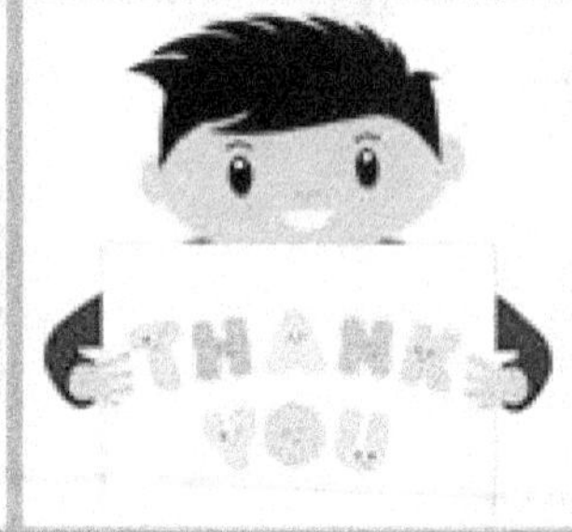	He made a Thank you card for you.
their	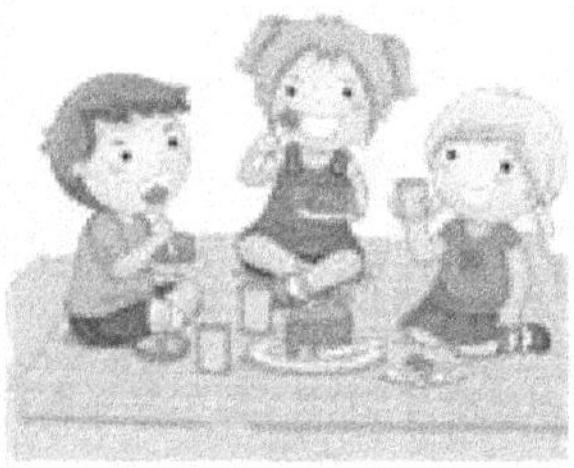	They will enjoy their picnic.
there	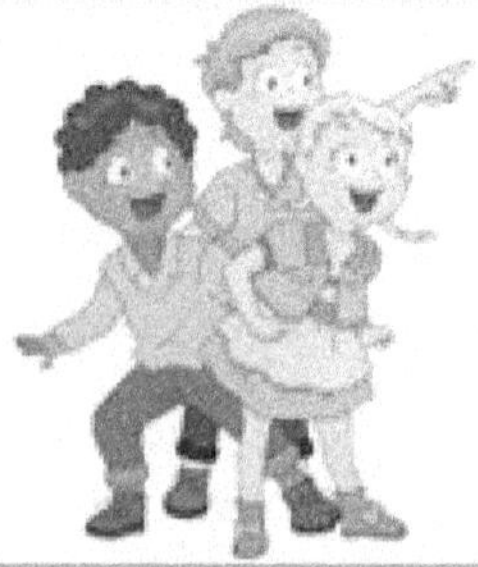	There is something in front of you.
these	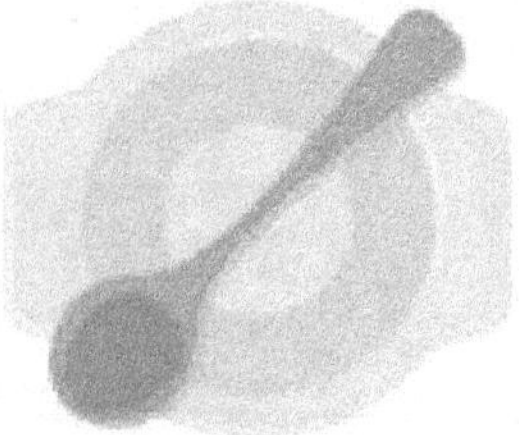	These are my eating material.
thing	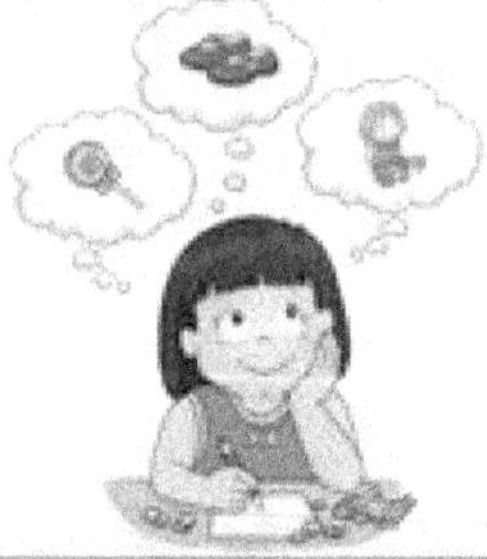	The thing is broken.
think	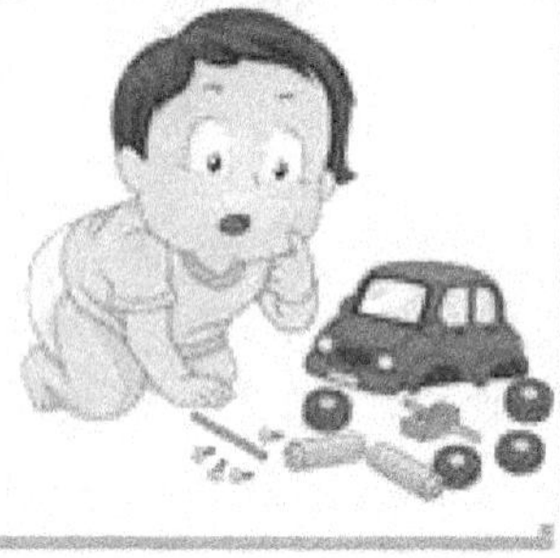	She thinks about what she is going to draw.

Read
Trace
Write
those
તે
three
ત્રણ
today
આજે
under
હેઠળ
watch
જુઓ
water
પાણી

Read and write the sentence!

Word		Sentence
those		Those are mine.
three		She will turn three today.
today		Today is a beautiful day.
under		The puppy sleeps under the blanket.
watch		They both watch the video.
water		He is drinking water after a long soccer game.

Read
Trace
Write
where
જ્યાં
which
જે
white
સફેદ
would
કરશે
write
લખો
always
હંમેશા

Read and write the sentence!

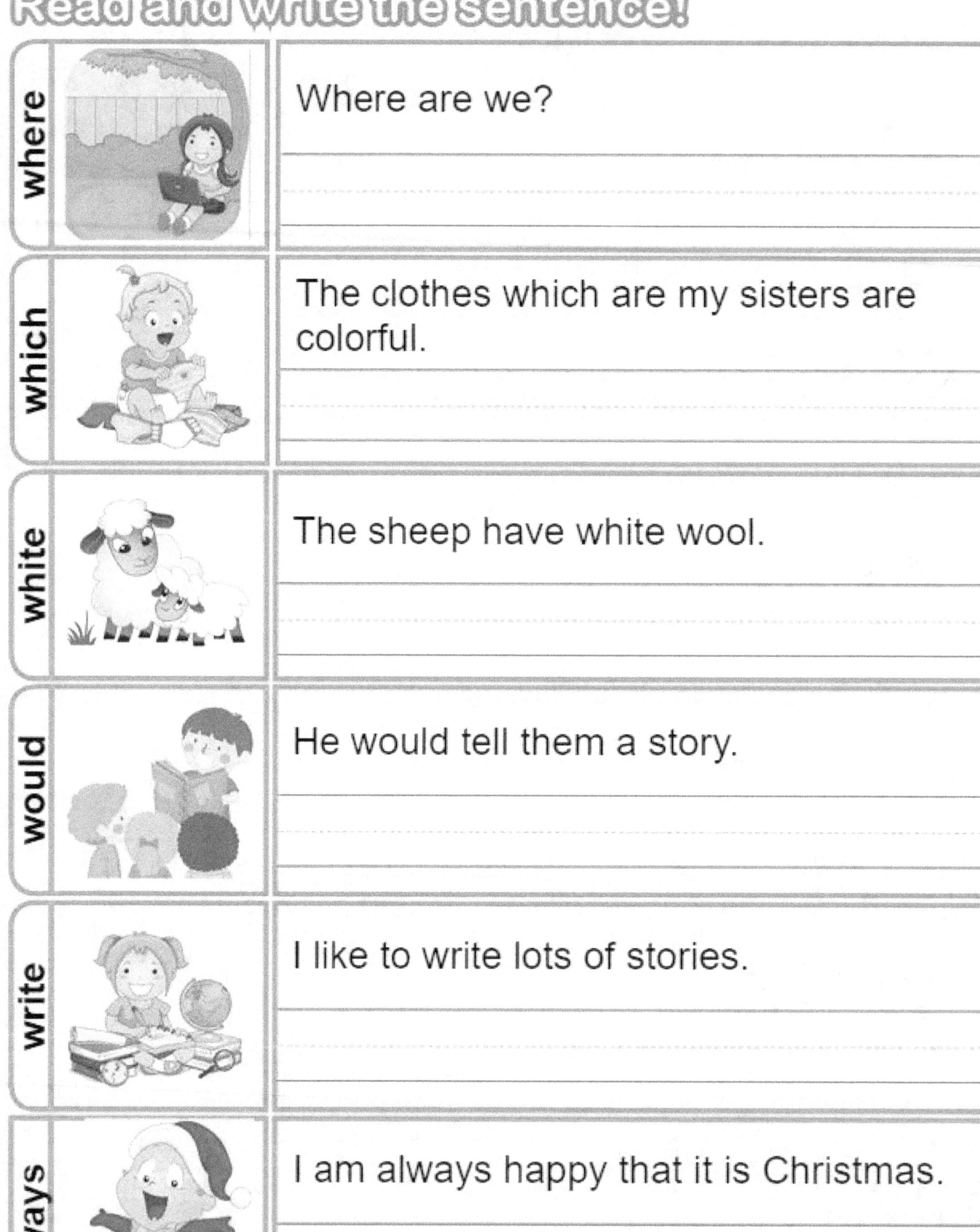

Read
Trace
Write

around
આસપાસ

before
પહેલાં

better
વધુ સારું

farmer
ખેડૂત

father
પિતા

flower
ફૂલ

Read and write the sentence!

around	I will shuffle the shapes around.
before	Before I go to school, I kiss my mom.
better	I can make it better.
farmer	The farmer takes care of the animals.
father	My father is wearing a blue shirt.
flower	She will play with the flowers.

Read	Trace	Write
garden બગીચો		
ground જમીન		
letter અક્ષરો		
little થોડું		
mother માતા		
myself મારી જાતને		

Read and write the sentence!

garden	Her garden is vast and healthy.
ground	I am playing with my dog on the ground.
letter	These are the letters A, B, and C.
little	The world is small.
mother	My mother is very nice.
myself	I made these by myself.

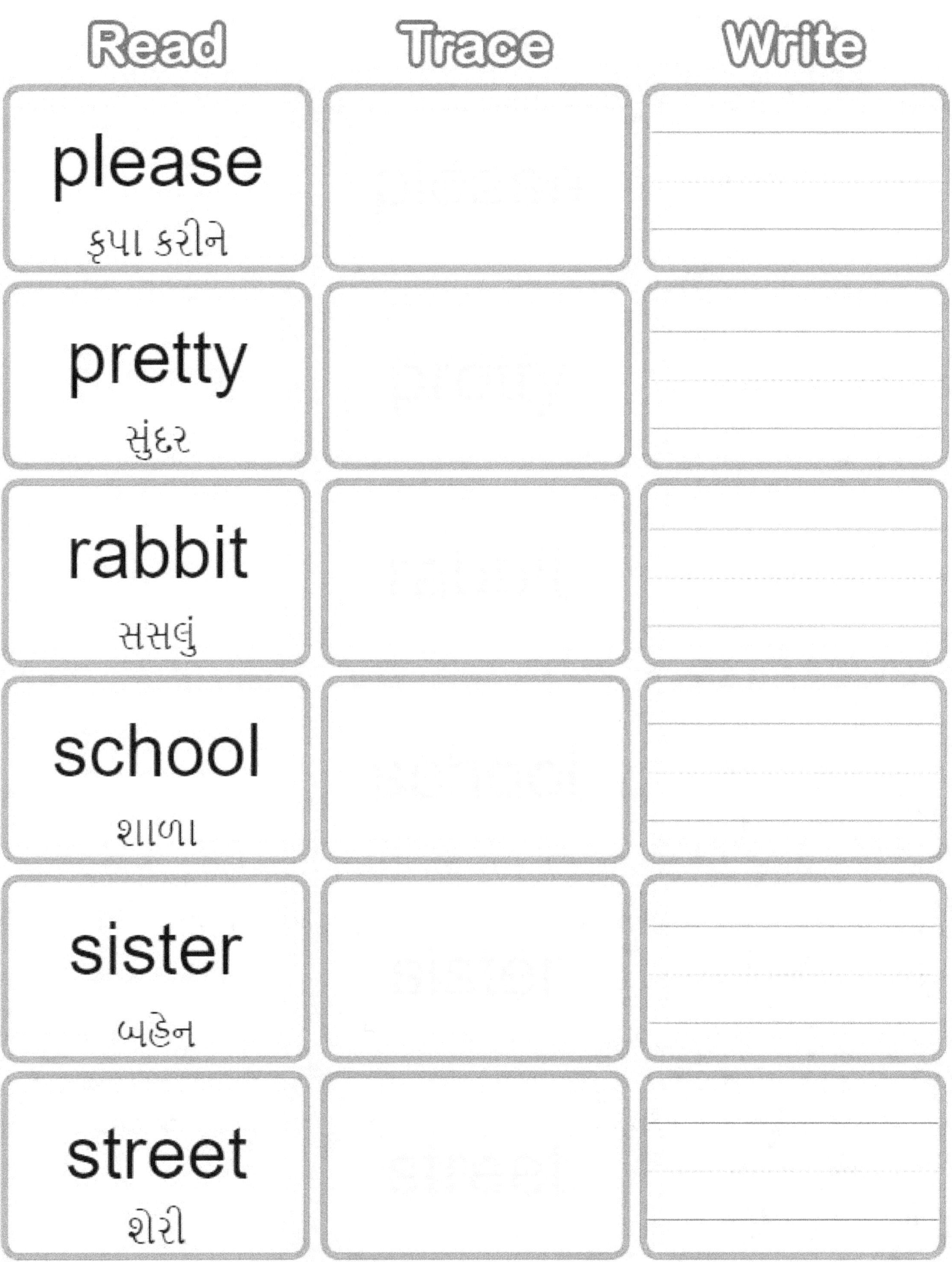

Read
Trace
Write
please
કૃપા કરીને
pretty
સુંદર
rabbit
સસલું
school
શાળા
sister
બ્હેન
street
શેરી

Read and write the sentence!

please	Please stop pulling my hair.
pretty	She made the cake very pretty.
rabbit	The rabbit is white and soft.
school	This is the school.
sister	My sister is wearing a pink dress.
street	They are walking across the street.

Read	Trace	Write
window વિંડો		
yellow પીળો		
because કારણ કે		
brother ભાઈ		
chicken ચિકન		
goodbye આવજો		

Read and write the sentence!

window — The window is open.

yellow — The ducky is yellow.

because — She will sleep because it is night.

brother — His brother is playing with him.

chicken — The chicken has hatched out of the egg.

goodbye — The animal is saying goodbye.

Read	Trace	Write
morning સવારે		
picture ચિત્ર		
birthday જન્મદિવસ		
children બાળકો		
squirrel ખિસકોલી		
together સાથે		

Read and write the sentence!

morning		He likes to ride his bike in the morning.
picture		He will take a picture.
birthday		Today is my birthday!
children		The children are doing something.
squirrel		The squirrel is cute.
together		They are sharing a bed together.

www.ingramcontent.com/pod-product-compliance
Lightning Source LLC
Chambersburg PA
CBHW080718120726
48001CB00010B/3064